THE RAILWAY STATION

PHILIPPE DUPASQUIER

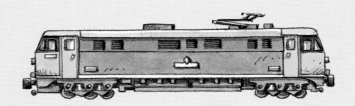

WALKER BOOKS
LONDON

It's early morning on East Side Station.
Winston Quickstep, the station inspector,
comes to wind the clock.

'There's plenty of time to buy my ticket,' thinks Brian Gurner on the way to visit his girlfriend.

The rush hour begins.
The first trains arrive.
Passengers begin to fill the station.

'Downhill-on-Sea,' says Brian.
'Single or return?' asks the booking clerk.
'Return,' Brian says firmly.

Alfred collects the tickets.
'Oh no!' says John Scales when his
briefcase bursts open.

'Push and shove, it's always the same at this hour of the morning,' Winston remarks to Brian.

Now it's mid-morning.
There is mail to unload on Platform four.
Lewis works as quickly as only Lewis can.

'Which way to the ski train?' Peter asks.
'Platform one, behind you,' Winston answers.
The sweet machine jams and Roger wrestles with it.

RRRRRRRRRROOAARRR! The train pulls out.
Whack! Peter turns round.

'Jackpot!' Roger shouts.
'Grrr!' Ginger grabs a feather.

In mid-afternoon a steam train arrives.
A film is being shot on the station.

'It's Marilyn Moonlight, the actress,' says
Maurice. 'Do you know she's forty-seven?'

The film is called *Good-bye Darling*.
'Action!' shouts the director, and the
camera starts to roll.

'Isn't she beautiful? The engine, I mean,'
says the man in the front row.
'Shhh!' whispers Winston. 'You'll spoil the film.'

Late in the day, an empty train is backed in.
'I don't believe it!' says John Scales,
having trouble with his briefcase again.

The last people in the queue will have to hurry because the train doesn't wait for long.
Alan quickly phones his wife.

'Only the first three coaches go to your station, miss,' says Alfred.

Winston checks his watch.
'I must dash now, darling,' says Alan.
'The train is about to leave.'